Top Secret

by Philippa Werry

Contents

CAMBRIDGE
UNIVERSITY PRESS

Prologue

World War I ended in 1918. Millions of people had been killed in four years of fighting. People hoped this would be "The War To End All Wars." Yet only 21 years later, the world was engulfed in another terrible war. How did that happen?

Germany was defeated in World War I. But the Nazi Party, led by Adolf Hitler, came to power in 1933. Hitler wanted to build an **empire** that would stretch across Europe. He made an **alliance** with Italy and took over German-speaking territory in Austria and Czechoslovakia.

On 1 September 1939, German troops marched into Poland. Two days later, Britain and France declared war on Germany. By the middle of 1940, Hitler had invaded much of Europe. The Luftwaffe (German Air Force) was bombing England in the Battle of Britain. Nobody knew how the war was going to end.

Bombers over London

Adolf Hitler

Map of Europe (June 1940) showing areas under German control

The S.O.E.

In July 1940, Winston Churchill, the British Prime Minister, gave orders to establish a top-secret organisation called the Special Operations Executive, or SOE. The job of the SOE was to bring down Hitler's Europe from the inside by carrying out acts of **sabotage** behind enemy lines. Or as Churchill put it, "to set Europe ablaze!"

Sabotaged bridge

Winston Churchill

Because it was a secret organisation, the SOE recruited by word of mouth. Agents came from all walks of life. Some were bankers or lawyers before joining the organisation. Others were teachers, railway workers, police or waiters. Some were even burglars or safebreakers just out of prison.

Anyone who was going to be a secret agent had to be very fit, both mentally and physically. It also helped to be fluent in a second language. The work was hard, lonely and often dangerous. Agents underwent rigorous tests and training to make sure they wouldn't crack under the strain.

Anyone who was offered a job was informed of the risks. Many agents did not survive the war. People knew that if they agreed to sign up, it could be a life-or-death decision.

By 1944, the staff of the SOE had grown to include 10,000 men and 3,000 women. Of these, about half of the men and 100 of the women worked behind enemy lines as secret agents. The rest of the staff worked behind the scenes doing work to support agents in the field.

An agent wires explosives to a railway track.

Do you have what it takes?

Secret agents needed to be:

- **Brave**
  About one in four agents were killed over the course of the war.

- **Loyal**
  A double agent could endanger many lives.

- **Patient**
  The life of a secret agent was not all action and excitement. Agents also had to cope with long periods of boredom and loneliness.

- **Observant**
  Agents had to be aware of what was going on around them at all times.

- **Practical**
  Agents had to be good at everything from map reading and riding a bicycle to handling weapons and operating radios.

- **Intelligent**
  A good secret agent had to be able to think two or three moves ahead all the time and not act impulsively.

Training

Before they were sent into occupied Europe, agents received training in the English countryside. Training took anything from ten weeks to ten months, depending on how much time was available. Not everyone finished the course. Some people were weeded out. Others decided the work was not for them.

All agents were given a new name and a new **identity**. They had to forget their old identity and invent a whole new background for themselves.

Agents in training

Combat training

Equipment

The secret agents who went behind enemy lines needed maps, clothing, and documents such as ID cards and ration cards. They also needed everyday items such as money, cigarettes and even pretend letters from made-up family members.

Maps

Agents were often sent into unknown territory, and they had to be able to find their way around. At the start of the war, there weren't many maps available so SOE staff had to make their own. They copied maps from books, magazines and textbooks. Sometimes they drew their own maps with the help of people who had lived in the area. Later in the war, they created maps from photographs taken from planes.

Secret agents working behind the scenes

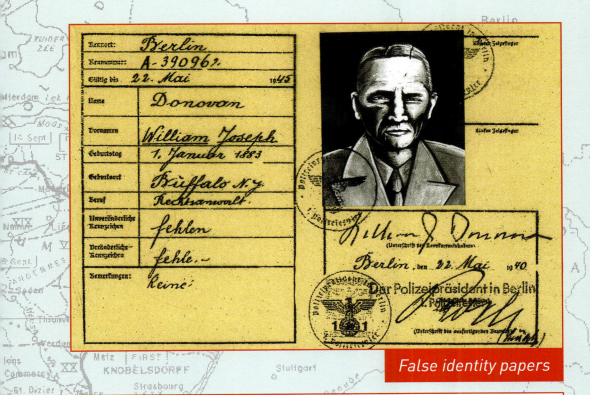

Documents

During the war, people in Europe had to carry ID and ration cards. ID cards made it easier for the occupying forces to determine who people were. Ration cards allowed people to buy food, which was often in short supply. Agents needed documents to be perfect copies of real ones. SOE staff made **counterfeit** documents by copying ones that had been stolen or smuggled out of Europe.

Money

Money was also smuggled out of Europe or counterfeited. Because crisp new notes or shiny coins might cause suspicion, the counterfeit money had to be aged. Notes were dipped in black dye and hung up to dry. Before they dried completely, the notes were scrunched up to make them look worn and crinkled.

Clothing

To survive **undercover**, it was important that the agents didn't stand out in any way. They had to wear clothes that looked just like everyone else's in Europe. SOE staff hunted through second-hand shops and bought clothes from European refugees.

When they couldn't find used clothes, SOE staff made new ones copying the styles being warn in Europe. Since not many people owned brand new clothing during the war, the SOE staff had to age the clothing they made to make it look more convincing.

To do this, an agent might put on a new suit and wear it for a week without taking it off. The agent would wear the suit to bed as well as when he showered. The creases were marked with Vaseline and dusted with something called rotten stone. Fine sandpaper was used to take the gloss off the lapels. Using these methods, a new suit could be made to look six months old.

SOE staff made clothing for undercover agents.

Gadgets

In addition to everyday items, the SOE designed and built a whole range of gadgets for their secret agents to use to carry out their assignments.

Spy Cameras

The SOE made tiny cameras and hid them inside cigarette lighters, buttons, pipes, pens, golf balls and hairbrushes.

Spy camera

Shaving brush with hidden compartment

Hidden Compartments

The SOE designed shaving cream canisters and toothbrush tubes with hidden compartments. Agents could safely hide secret messages or other objects in what looked like ordinary bathroom supplies. If the object needed to be kept dry, it was placed inside a balloon.

An SOE agent draws maps on playing cards. Maps were also hidden inside records, which needed to be broken to reveal the map.

Invisible Maps and Edible Notepaper

Some maps were printed in invisible ink on handkerchiefs. The ink had to be soaked in urine before it could be read.

The SOE printed other maps on fine tissue paper, rolled them round soft wire and tied them with cotton ties. These maps were no more than three millimetres in diameter and would fit inside an ordinary pencil.

Agents carried edible notepaper made out of rice paper. If an agent got caught by enemy forces, he could eat top-secret information before it fell into enemy hands.

Exploding Pencils, Rats and Turds

The time pencil was a time-delay device that let an agent light an explosive, but have time to escape before it went off. When the agent pressed a ridge on the pencil, acid was released and started to eat through a wire attached to a **detonator**. Twelve million of these were produced during the war.

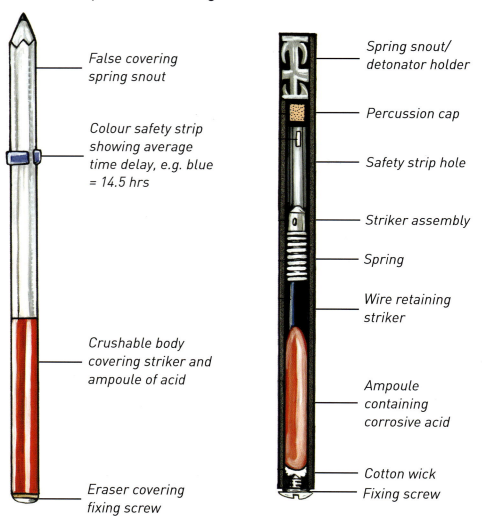

False covering spring snout

Colour safety strip showing average time delay, e.g. blue = 14.5 hrs

Crushable body covering striker and ampoule of acid

Eraser covering fixing screw

Spring snout/ detonator holder

Percussion cap

Safety strip hole

Striker assembly

Spring

Wire retaining striker

Ampoule containing corrosive acid

Cotton wick

Fixing screw

A diagram of the outside and inside of an exploding pencil

The dead bodies of real rats were stuffed with plastic explosives. The idea was to put them in the pile of coal near the boiler of a ship, steam train, or factory. When they were shovelled into the boiler, they would explode.

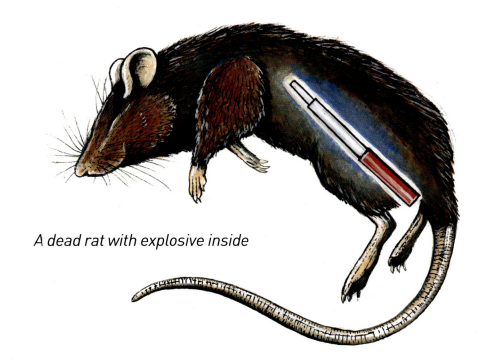

A dead rat with explosive inside

Almost as strange was the exploding turd. These were imitation horse, donkey, cow or camel turds with an explosive filling. They were designed to be placed on the road and fired by a pressure switch when a tank or car went over them.

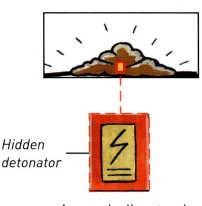

Hidden detonator

An exploding turd

Behind Enemy Lines

After finishing training, agents parachuted behind enemy lines. There they did anything they could to undermine the enemy. Agents carried out acts of sabotage. They blew up bridges, power plants, and train tracks. Not all of the activities of secret agents were violent. For example, some agents used forged documents to send enemy supply trains to the wrong locations.

Agents also gathered information about the enemy's activities. Agents had wireless radios that they could use to send coded messages back to Britain. This was very important, but dangerous work. If a transmission took too long, the agent could get caught.

It's estimated that about 200 agents lost their lives during World War II. Adolf Hitler gave orders to execute any agents that were captured. Each agent carried two sets of pills. When agents needed to stay awake, they took Benzedrine. The 'L' tablet was a suicide pill that the agent could take in case of capture. If the agent bit down on it, he would be dead in 15 seconds.

Bombed bridge

Violette Szabo: Female Agent

Violette Bushell was born in Paris in 1921. Her father was English, but her mother was French. She spent much of her childhood in France and could speak the language perfectly.

When war broke out, Violette was living with her family in London. In 1940, she met and fell in love with a French officer, Etienne Szabo. The two of them were married, but Etienne did not live to see his daughter's birth. He was killed in battle in October 1942.

After her husband's death, Violette was determined to do something to help the war effort. Aware of the dangers involved, she joined the SOE.

Violette was sent to France in April 1944. Her assignment was to check on **Resistance groups** in an area that was full of German troops.

Violette Szabo

A concentration camp in Germany

Violette had to use all her wits to collect information while avoiding capture herself. She was often stopped and her papers examined, but each time she managed to talk herself out of trouble.

Violette returned to England, but she was sent back to France in June 1944. A few days into her mission she and a companion were stopped at a German road block. Violette held off the Germans with gunfire, giving her companion time to escape. She was captured and **interrogated**, but refused to say anything. Later Violette was sent to a concentration camp. She was executed in February 1945.

Epilogue

Adolf Hitler committed suicide on 30 April 1945. The war ended in Europe a few days later on 8 May. Atom bombs were dropped on the Japanese cities of Hiroshima and Nagasaki in early August 1945. Japan surrendered on 2 September 1945. World War II was over. More than 50 million people had been killed.

The SOE was dissolved in January 1946. But what impact did it have on the outcome of the war? Secret agents carried out acts of sabotage, such as blowing up bridges, and helped to organise local Resistance groups. Most importantly, they brought hope into the darkness of war, and showed the people of occupied countries that they had not been forgotten. They fought for freedom and often paid for it with their lives.

Crowd after the announcement of the end of the war

Glossary

alliance   an agreement to work together

counterfeit   something that is fake, but made to look like the real thing

detonator   a device that sets off an explosion

empire   a group of countries that has the same ruler

identity   who you are

interrogated   to be asked questions

Resistance group   a secret organisation that fights authority in an occupied country

sabotage   to intentionally destroy property

undercover   doing secret work

Index